THE
BIG WHY

WHY DO BAD THINGS HAPPEN TO GOOD PEOPLE?

REV. DR. DAVID HENION

THE BIG WHY
WHY DO BAD THINGS HAPPEN TO GOOD PEOPLE?

Author Credit: Rev. Dr. David Henion

iUniverse books may be ordered through booksellers or by contacting:

iUniverse
1663 Liberty Drive
Bloomington, IN 47403
www.iuniverse.com
1-800-Authors (1-800-288-4677)

Because of the dynamic nature of the internet, any web addresses or links contained in this book may have changed since publication and may no longer be valid. The views expressed in this work are solely those of the author and do not necessarily reflect the views of the publisher, and the publisher hereby disclaims any responsibility for them.

Any people depicted in stock imagery provided by Getty Images are models, and such images are being used for illustrative purposes only. Certain stock imagery © Getty Images.

ISBN: 978-1-5320-6661-0 (sc)
ISBN: 978-1-5320-6660-3 (e)

Library of Congress Control Number: 2019901026

Print information available on the last page.

iUniverse rev. date: 03/08/2019

Contents

INTRODUCTION

I wanted to write on this topic from a biblical perspective to help make sense out of some of the most tragic and seemingly senseless events of this life. I hope to comfort, strengthen, and encourage the families and friends who have walked through some of these confusing incidents.

I think of the father who, out of consideration for his tired wife, took his six-week-premature baby out of her crib because she was crying at 2:15 a.m. He brought her into the living room, lay on the couch, placed her on his chest, and got her to settle down. They both fell asleep until he woke up at 7:12 to find her underneath his body, accidentally suffocated.

I think of the family, colleagues, and friends of the officer murdered in cold blood while answering a false call the perpetrator had set up to kill an officer in the line of duty.

I think of the spouse of a newlywed killed in a car wreck or the parents of a child who was to graduate from high school the morning he was found dead from an aneurysm. I think of the many parents, spouses, children, and siblings who have watched life snatched away from a loved one. My prayer is that this book will help bring relief.

This is also written for all military, police, fire, EMS, and emergency room professionals who respond to and deal with painful aspects of life every day. As they try to make sense of these tragedies, I hope to help them understand their special call in dealing with the ugly events of this fallen world.

Even those who have a deep faith can find themselves struggling with the whys. Those who believe in a sovereign, all-powerful, all-present, all-knowing, wise, kind, holy, and loving God can wonder how He would allow the tragedy, especially if He has the power to stop it. None of it seems to make sense.

Many great thinkers, philosophers, and theologians have tried to answer the perplexing and fundamental questions of life. One of those questions is, of course, "Why do bad things happen to good people?" Rabbi Harold Kushner wrote a book with that title as he walked through his own personal tragedy after losing a young son to premature-aging syndrome. He has walked a hard personal road, and our prayers go out for him and his wife.

In the process of thinking about an omnipotent and benevolent God, Rabbi Kushner concluded that God must be powerful but that, rather than being a good and loving God, He must be a cruel God who allows such events to take place. This God gives good people suffering and pain. He could prevent this, but instead, He watches them suffer and struggle. Otherwise, God must not be powerful and is unable to prevent suffering. He must be a weak and ineffective God who loves but has no control.

I can understand Rabbi Kushner's conclusions, but I find them far from what the scriptures say. Thus, I chose to write this book to provide a biblical understanding of this emotionally charged and intellectually and spiritually challenging issue.

A key to understanding this involves what happened at the beginning of time and the curse that has hung over humanity for all generations since. We receive information about this from God's message through the apostle Paul's book of Romans, which was written to explain Christianity to the Christians in Rome.

CHAPTER 1

The Curse

The apostle Paul wrote the book of Romans as a summary of Christian doctrine to the people of Rome. It is a sweeping book that covers God's saving history of the world. He begins with humans' sinful nature. He artfully shares how God had a plan to save us, and then he follows with the application of how saved Christian men and women live in this world as children of God.

In the heart of Romans, Paul deals with suffering as the Christian lives the life as a special child of God. He gives us a lot of understanding in this area as one who experienced unjust suffering for his faith. In Romans 8:18–30, he gives the foundation for suffering in the world as it was then and is right now, and he gives answers to this hard question. Let's look at what he says and trace his logic:

> I consider that the sufferings of this present time are not worth comparing

> with the glory that is to be revealed to us.
> (Romans 8:18 RSV)

He recognizes that there are some harsh situations in life. Even though the pain in this life is tough and life can give us some terrible tragedies, it is nothing compared to the great and glorious life the believer has waiting in heaven with God. It is hard for some to understand, but this life will never give us full satisfaction.

> For the creation waits with eager longing
> for the revealing of the sons of God.
> (Romans 8:19 RSV)

Paul is saying that all of creation cannot wait for the final change that will come when Jesus comes back to remake creation. He will deliver it from the bondage of this curse it is under right now. In the next couple of verses, he amplifies even more about this bondage and futility that it is subject to:

> For the creation was subjected to futility,
> not of its own will but by the will of him
> who subjected it in hope; because the
> creation itself will be set free from its
> bondage to decay and obtain the glorious
> liberty of the children of God. We know
> that the whole creation has been groaning
> in travail together until now; and not
> only the creation, but we ourselves, who
> have the first fruits of the Spirit, groan

> inwardly as we wait for adoption as sons,
> the redemption of our bodies. (Romans
> 8:20–23 RSV)

Paul comes to the point of suffering in this world and the realization that this world is under a curse called *sin*. Sin put us in bondage and causes all kinds of ugly things to happen to men and women—both inwardly and outwardly. Sin causes all kinds of physical ailments, including cancer, viruses, diseases, and Alzheimer's disease. It also causes hatred, murder, greed, and devastation. These are part of human nature because of sin.

How is the world under such a curse? For that answer, we must go back to the beginning of God's creation and to our first parents: Adam and Eve.

CHAPTER 2

The Curse That Makes Us Cry and Curse

In the beginning, everything that was created by God was good.

> And God saw everything that he had made, and behold, it was very good. (Genesis 1:31a RSV)

With the creation of Adam and Eve, he also gave them a stipulation:

> But the Lord God warned him, "You may freely eat the fruit of every tree in the garden—except the tree of the knowledge of good and evil. If you eat its fruit, you are sure to die." (Genesis 2:16–17 NLT)

Satan tempted Eve to disregard what God said and got her to partake of the fruit along with Adam (Genesis 3:1–3). Satan uses a trick that still works today. He gets her to doubt what God says:

> "You won't die!" the serpent replied to the woman. "God knows that your eyes will be opened as soon as you eat it, and you will be like God, knowing both good and evil." (Genesis 2:4–6 NLT)

He claims that God doesn't want you to have what He has because you will be equal to Him. Both Eve and Adam fell for it, and the curse of sin entered the world (Genesis 3:6).

Sin means rebellion or setting ourselves up as gods by thinking we know more than God does. It is missing the mark that God set. Sin can be defined as the middle letter "I" that wants and takes control. *I* don't need God. *I* am the master of my destiny. *I* don't have to listen or obey Him because *I* know what *I* need. *I* don't need His help.

When Adam and Eve partook of the fruit, everything on earth was changed in a negative way. Things will not be made right until Christ returns to redo heaven and earth.

First, humanity's relationship with God was hurt deeply. Their rebellion, fear, and guilt affected their relationships with God. They had failed God miserably and were afraid to meet with God, which was tragic. Before that event, it was free, fun, uninhibited, and open for them to visit with and stand before God. But that changed, and they hid from God (Genesis 3:8).

Eating of the fruit brought a new awareness and a closing of the heart, mind, body, and soul to vulnerability, freedom, and openness in the world. God knew what had taken place with Adam and Eve. They were afraid and ashamed of their nakedness, and God asked them if they had eaten the fruit (Genesis 3:9–11).

Honesty went out the window with the fall, and finding someone else to blame for one's guilt became the norm. Adam blamed Eve. Eve blamed the serpent, and God held them all accountable. Through the one sin of disobedience, the universe and the world were affected with the curse that spread like cancer (Genesis 3:12–13).

God gave the serpent, Satan, His judgment and punishment. He cursed the serpent, and it would grovel on its belly all its life (Genesis 3:14).

Satan would always be at odds with humans and would harass humankind. At the end of the verse, God prophesizes about His coming in the flesh, as Jesus, who Satan would hurt in this life with suffering and pain as He goes to the cross. However, Jesus would defang Satan by striking his head and taking away the curse of sin, which is eternal death (Genesis 3:15).

> Then God speaks to the woman. The curse meted out to Eve would also pass on to all women in the act of giving birth. Now women would experience pain in childbirth, "Then he said to the woman, 'I will sharpen the pain of your pregnancy,

> and in pain you will give birth.'" (Genesis 3:16 NLT)

> Also conflict between men and women in their marriage relationships will take place. A battle for power and control, "And you will desire to control your husband, but he will rule over you." (Genesis 3:16b NLT)

Humanity's relationship to work, which was meant as an enjoyable experience in the perfect creation before the fall, had been turned into difficult labor. It would be a battle:

> The ground is cursed because of you. All your life you will struggle to scratch a living from it. It will grow thorns and thistles for you, though you will eat of its grains. By the sweat of your brow will you have food to eat. (Genesis 17b–19a NLT)

Death from all kinds of diseases and tragedies is also introduced into the picture. It would be passed on to all generations to come because Eve was the mother of all who live:

> Until you return to the ground from which you were made. For you were made from dust, and to dust you will return. Then the man—Adam—named his wife Eve,

> because she would be the mother of all
> who live. (Genesis 19b–20 NLT)

This curse affects all people. Both good and evil people would live under it, according to Jesus:

> For he makes his sun rise on the evil and
> on the good, and sends rain on the just
> and on the unjust. (Matthew 5:45b RSV)

Also, honesty and vulnerability would be taken away from relationships, and it would be hard to keep that going. Men and women would be covered up, hiding, and deceiving each other:

> And the Lord God made clothing from
> animal skins for Adam and his wife.
> (Genesis 3:21 RSV)

All kinds of evil were introduced with the fall of Adam and Eve. Wickedness and evil would be brought by others unto others—whether it was personal or with groups of people. We see the first murder in a very unlikely situation.

In the context of a very spiritual experience of giving gifts to God in worship, the horrific sin of murder first takes place between Adam and Eve's sons (Genesis 4:3–7). Due to Cain's anger and jealousy—because his brother's offering was accepted by God and his wasn't—he lets it get the best of him. With his sinful cursed nature taking control of him, Cain kills his brother (Genesis 4:8).

Humanity is cursed in being very capable perpetuators of all kinds of evil.

In this cursed and fallen world, even the righteous and good will not always see justice. Good doesn't always win. Paul warns Timothy, as a church leader, to realize that along with all the people of this world.

> Yes, and all who desire to live godly in Christ Jesus will suffer persecution. But evil men and impostors will grow worse and worse, deceiving and being deceived. (2 Timothy 3:12–13 RSV)

Sadly, in this world, evil will triumph for a season. God's people have been persecuted and killed through the centuries for doing God's goodwill. It will go from bad to worse at times. This was nothing new to the church because Jesus had warned His disciples before His death:

> These things I have spoken to you, that in Me you may have peace. In the world you will have tribulation; but be of good cheer, I have overcome the world. (John 16:33 NASV)

It is a reality that good Christians will suffer for their faith, and it is a vivid reminder of the curse the world is under.

This sinful nature leads individuals and nations to sin against each other for evil reasons (James 4:1–3). Nations go to war for many reasons, and a lot of them are not pure. The resources a nation has that another wants, an ethnic or religious hatred, or a desire to dominate or enslave are a few examples.

The devil's pride got him to rebel against God in heaven, and it got him thrown out to wait until his final judgment of being sent to hell, and so will it be for mankind (Isaiah 14:14–15).

Humans—by doubting God's Word, refusing to obey, showing lustful pride, and wanting to be like God—sinned and rebelled against God and were tossed out of the Garden of Eden (Genesis 3:22–23). Now, all of humanity is under the curse and will not live in the beautiful, pure, and good existence of the Garden of Eden (Genesis 3:24) until the second coming of the Lord. It will bring a new heaven and a new earth—with the joy, beauty, and satisfaction that was Eden (Revelation 21:1). The apostle John describes it as a place where we will be with God, and all the ugly diseases, pain, and suffering will be no more (Revelation 21:3–4). The evil unrepentant we see on this earth will be sent to their judgment in hell, and justice will fully reign (Revelation 21:8). They will join the devil who will be thrown into hell just before the new heaven and new earth are made (Revelation 20:1–3).

So here we have seen it. All this death, pain, suffering, hatred, and murder has come because our first parents' rebellion dearly cost humanity and the world:

> For as in Adam all die, so also in Christ all will be made alive. (1 Corinthians 15:22 NASV)

In the meantime, we live in this beautiful world that is marred by the curse and is fallen. Humans are fallen and sinful—religious and nonreligious, moral, immoral, and pagan:

> For all have sinned and fall short of the glory of God. (Romans 3:23 NASV)

No one can earn his or her way to heaven on their own. They must be perfect.

> You, therefore, must be perfect, as your heavenly Father is perfect. (Matthew 5:48 RSV)

If humans could do it on their own, they could brag about it:

> Not because of works, lest any man should boast. (Ephesians 2:9 RSV)

We can't do it on our own. The wages we get for sinfulness is death:

> For the wages of sin is death, but the free gift of God is eternal life in Christ Jesus our Lord. (Romans 6:23 RSV)

But our gracious and merciful God provided a way to save us by sending His Son who lived the perfect life and became the sacrifice for our sins:

> For by grace you have been saved through
> faith; and this is not your own doing, it is
> the gift of God. (Ephesians 2:8 RSV)

When we are saved and trust Christ, we are on a faith journey. We trust God in all kinds of good and bad events in life. We trust that He will bring us through them in the process of sanctification. He uses the circumstance to conform us to the likeness of Jesus. We see this as we go back to Romans 8 and finish out the challenging issue for good Christians who ask God why as they go through difficulties as they try to live obedient lives for Him.

CHAPTER 3

The Purpose of the Curse for God's Children

Paul speaks about hope and faith. With the right disposition of the heart toward God—even though we can't see how or what is going to happen—we can trust God with the way it will turn out.

> For in this hope we were saved. Now hope
> that is seen is not hope. For who hopes for
> what he sees? But if we hope for what we
> do not see, we wait for it with patience.
> (Romans 8:24–25 RSV)

It is the patient trust in God he is speaking of, which is faith. If we knew how it was going to turn out, it wouldn't take hope or faith. It would be a sure thing.

Paul speaks about God's provision of the Holy Spirit who helps us in the struggle of faith and brings comfort in our pains and doubts:

> Likewise the Spirit helps us in our weakness; for we do not know how to pray as we ought, but the Spirit himself intercedes for us with sighs too deep for words. (Romans 8:26 RSV)

He understands our pain, struggles, and doubt better than we do. He intercedes for us even when we can't put our hurt and pain into words. We also are told the Holy Spirit cleans up our requests and makes them line up with the will of God:

> And he who searches the hearts of men knows what is the mind of the Spirit, because the Spirit intercedes for the saints according to the will of God. (Romans 8:27 RSV)

> We know that in everything God works for good with those who love him, who are called according to his purpose. (Romans 8:28 RSV)

He says "everything" that happens in our lives is for our good. We struggle with that kind of thinking when it comes to circumstances that are, at times, overwhelmingly negative in our lives.

We often ask, "Where's the good?" Notice the two qualifiers he uses: "with those who love Him," and "who are called according to His purpose." This makes no sense to those who don't love God wholeheartedly and are not called by God for salvation.

With God not being the first and primary source of life and destiny, His will means nothing. However, when God's will is the utmost priority in one's life, then God's desire becomes one's utmost interest. What is that? He says what it is in the next verse:

> For those whom he foreknew he also predestined to be conformed to the image of his Son, in order that he might be the first-born among many brethren. (Romans 8:29 RSV)

He saves us so that we may be "conformed to the image of His Son." That's God's will! There is nothing that can be greater than to be the kind of God glorifier that Christ was as He walked this earth.

Paul reveals how God does this:

> And those whom he predestined he also called; and those whom he called he also justified; and those whom he justified he also glorified. (Romans 8:30 RSV)

For Christians, this is our real experience. Is this what we were made to be? One of the confessions of the church asks, "What is the chief end of humanity?"

To glorify God and enjoy Him forever!

CHAPTER 4

The Purpose for Good

This process of glorification was not foreign to the early believers. We see this with James and the other early apostles:

> Count it all joy, my brethren, when you
> meet various trials, for you know that the
> testing of your faith produces steadfastness.
> And let steadfastness have its full effect,
> that you may be perfect and complete,
> lacking in nothing. (James 1:2–4 RSV)

The believers of James's day were scattered throughout Asia Minor because of the trials and persecutions the Christians experienced. James speaks of joy not as an emotion but as a deep-seated fruit of the Holy Spirit that comes with trusting God. It is the assurance that they know God is purposely working in them to build a steadfastness that brings a deep maturity in sharing in the suffering that Christ endured.

Peter gives us a similar explanation:

> In this you rejoice, though now for a little while you may have to suffer various trials, so that the genuineness of your faith, more precious than gold which though perishable is tested by fire, may redound to praise and glory and honor at the revelation of Jesus Christ. (1 Peter 1:6–7 RSV)

Peter understood this from firsthand experience. Peter, the self-made man, thought he could handle his walk as a disciple, but his prideful ego often got in the way. God had to break him so Peter would realize his need to depend on Christ alone. We see it when Jesus went to wash his feet and Peter first denied the Lord:

> Jesus answered him, "What I am doing you do not know now, but afterward you will understand." Peter said to him, "You shall never wash my feet." Jesus answered him, "If I do not wash you, you have no part in me." Simon Peter said to him, "Lord, not my feet only but also my hands and my head!" (John 13:7–9 RSV)

Peter seems to get it, but he still doesn't. Jesus loved Peter, but Peter needed to be put on God's sanctification program. Jesus had a plan to conform Peter to a right relationship with Him. To do this, Peter would need to have a trusting faith to trust Christ to carry him through the trials of ministry that he would face. Jesus told Peter it would happen:

> Simon, Satan has asked to sift you like wheat. (Luke 22:31 NLT)

After that, Jesus predicted that Peter would deny the Lord three times. And when Jesus was arrested, Peter did deny His Lord. Peter was at his lowest, and even though he saw the Lord after the resurrection, he didn't have a face-to-face with Him until Jesus challenged Peter about his love and ego. Jesus told him of his faith change:

> Truly, truly, I say to you, when you were young, you girded yourself and walked where you would; but when you are old, you will stretch out your hands, and another will gird you and carry you where you do not wish to go. This he said to show by what death he was to glorify God, And after this, He said to him, "Follow me." (John 21:18–19)

Scripture and tradition tell us that Peter was put through great persecution. We see some persecution he suffered in the book of Acts, but he also suffered later in his death.

In *The Master's Men: Character Sketches of the Disciples*, theologian William Barclay recounts that Peter watched his wife being tortured and crucified for following Jesus as the persecutors taunted Peter to recant his faith. His response was to encourage his wife by telling her to "remember the Lord." After she was crucified, he was put to the cross. He asked that he not be crucified straight up as the Lord was because he was unworthy to be crucified like Jesus his Lord. Therefore, he was crucified upside down.

The apostle Paul discusses the purpose of suffering extensively in his epistles. Paul writes about God working in his life to be conformed to the image of Christ.

> Therefore, since we are justified by faith, we have peace with God through our Lord Jesus Christ. Through him we have obtained access to this grace in which we stand, and we rejoice in our hope of sharing the glory of God. More than that, we rejoice in our sufferings, knowing that suffering produces endurance, and endurance produces character, and character produces hope, and hope does not disappoint us, because God's love has been poured into our hearts through the Holy Spirit which has been given to us. (Romans 5:1–4 RSV)

However, this is more than just an abstract idea for Paul. He lived it out in a physical way. Paul was dealing with a physical problem that continued to hamper him. He repeatedly prayed for God to remove it, yet God didn't heal him.

And to keep me from being too elated by the abundance of revelations, a thorn was given me in the flesh, a messenger of Satan, to harass me, to keep me from being too elated. Three times I besought the Lord about this, that it should leave me; but he said to me, "My grace is sufficient for you, for my power is made perfect in weakness." I will all the more gladly boast of my weaknesses, that the power of Christ may rest upon me. For the sake of Christ, then, I am content with weaknesses, insults, hardships, persecutions, and calamities; for when I am weak, then I am strong. (2 Corinthians 12:7–10 RSV)

Paul rejoiced in his weaknesses to glorify Christ.

CHAPTER 5

The Purpose of Testing: Genuine Faith

In the Old Testament book of Job, there is another case of evil befalling a godly and righteous man and his family—not because of any evil they had done but for being good. His friends tried to convince Job that the bad things happened because Job had sinned. However, that was not the case. In fact, it was just the opposite. Satan comes to God, who is proud of Job and the way he has walked with God:

> And the Lord said to Satan, "Have you considered my servant Job, that there is none like him on the earth, a blameless and upright man, who fears God and turns away from evil?" (Job 1:8 RSV)

Look at how Satan answers God about Job's goodness and righteousness. Satan postulates that Job was faithful because God has protected him and blessed him with a lot of good things and increased his wealth. Satan challenges God:

> Take it all away from Job and let's see how faithful, righteous and blameless he will be. He will curse you God. (Job 1:10 RSV)

God gives Satan the ability to work Job over to see how good his faith is when all is taken away. In all of this, Job remained faithful to God. Even though he struggled with the loss of family, wealth, and power, he still trusted God (Job 1:20–22).

Job's faith in God was not shaken, so Satan comes back to take away his health. The only limit God puts on Satan was that he could not kill Job. Satan then afflicts Job physically:

> So Satan went forth from the presence of the Lord, and afflicted Job with loathsome sores from the sole of his foot to the crown of his head. And he took a potsherd with which to scrape himself, and sat among the ashes. (Job 2:7–8 RSV)

Job's wife tells him to end his suffering by cursing God. Job's faith in God can be seen in response to her advice:

> Then his wife said to him, "Do you still hold fast your integrity? Curse God, and die." But he said to her, "You speak as one

> of the foolish women would speak. Shall
> we receive good at the hand of God, and
> shall we not receive evil?" In all this Job
> did not sin with his lips. (Job 2:9–10 RSV)

What a witness for generations to come! The most important thing in all of life is having God! God could give a person all the blessings, material things, and joys, but if He does not give us Himself, we have nothing. All the stuff, the experiences, and the joys of life are nothing compared to knowing God and having a relationship with Him.

Paul shares this lesson from his life:

> So we do not lose heart. Though our outer
> nature is wasting away, our inner nature
> is being renewed every day. For this slight
> momentary affliction is preparing for
> us an eternal weight of glory beyond all
> comparison, because we look not to the
> things that are seen but to the things that
> are unseen; for the things that are seen are
> transient, but the things that are unseen
> are eternal. (2 Corinthians 4:16–18 RSV)

Sometimes God allows difficult things to happen just to remind us of His ultimate value in our hearts. Not even the closest relationships on earth can compare to the ultimate place He should have in our hearts. Jesus spelled that out in the Sermon on the Mount:

> If any one comes to me and does not hate
> his own father and mother and wife and
> children and brothers and sisters, yes,
> and even his own life, he cannot be my
> disciple. (Luke 14:26 RSV)

Jesus explains, in a very strong way, that the wonderful God-given relationships we are to honor and love in this life would seem to be "hate" when compared to the ultimate love and value we are to give toward God.

In the Bible, suffering and death were considered a privilege by the saints of God. They were warned not to preach about Jesus and were beaten with whips:

> They went on their way from the presence
> of the Council, rejoicing that they had
> been considered worthy to suffer shame
> for His name. (Acts 5:41 NASB)

The book of Revelation mentions the special reward and place for sufferers and martyrs. God has a set number of those who would suffer and be killed through martyrdom before the end is to come:

> And there was given to each of them a
> white robe; and they were told that they
> should rest for a little while longer, until
> the number of their fellow servants and
> their brethren who were to be killed even
> as they had been, would be completed
> also. (Revelation 6:11 NASB)

CHAPTER 6

Suffering Is Also Used to Punish

Punishment is sometimes the first conclusion that comes to some Christians who have been brought up in a legalistic home of rules and regulations. As we saw with Job and the apostles, this is not always the case. However, there are times when suffering does come as punishment for sin and disobedience.

David was "a man after God's own heart" (1 Samuel 13:14 RSV). When a man of God sins, God does not fool around. Because of David's sin of adultery with Bathsheba—and then murdering her husband to cover it up—God came down on him hard. First, David saw the beautiful Bathsheba taking a bath on her roof and invited her to his palace, where they committed adultery. Because of their frolic, she became pregnant.

David tried to cover up the pregnancy by bringing her husband off the battlefield to sleep with her so they could claim the child was conceived with her husband.

Her honorable husband, Uriah, would not sleep with her while his troops were in the field and could not be with their wives. Instead, Uriah sleeps at the entrance to the palace. David tried a second time by getting him good and drunk, hoping he would go home and have relations with his wife, but he stayed at the palace with the other servants (2 Samuel 11:1–13).

David became desperate, and he hatched a plot with General Joab to murder Uriah. The plan was to get Uriah into a fierce battle. When the battle was most intense, Joab would give a signal for all the other soldiers to pull back, leaving Uriah by himself to be killed in the line of duty. It will be an honorable death, making him a military hero (2 Samuel 11:14–17). The plan was executed, and Uriah died. In truth, by his plan, David murdered Uriah.

God punished David as a leader—both personally and corporately. Even though David was forgiven, God made him deal with the natural consequences of his sins. Nathan, the prophet, confronts David in his own denial, and a beautiful word picture makes David realize what he has done. In 2 Samuel 12:1–4, Nathan tells the story of a man whose beloved sheep was robbed by a rich man. In reaction to hearing of the injustice, David demands the poor man be restored fourfold.

Nathan drops the punch on David that it was his adultery with Bathsheba and the murder of her husband (2 Samuel 12:5–9). Nathan goes on to list the consequences and punishments God is going to do so he can learn the lesson as a believer and a leader:

First, the sword would not depart from the house of David. "Now therefore the sword shall never depart from your house, because you have despised me, and have taken the wife of Uri'ah the Hittite to be your wife." (2 Samuel 12:10 RSV)

David lost three sons—Amnon, Absalom, and Adonijah—through death by sword. Absalom was murdered by General Joab because he tried to kill David and overthrow the kingdom. His long hair got caught up in a tree, and as he was hanging there, Joab did the deed—even though David didn't want him harmed.

"Enough of this nonsense," Joab said. Then he took three daggers and plunged them into Absalom's heart as he dangled, still alive, in the great tree. (2 Samuel 18:14 NLT)

Later, David's third son was murdered by Solomon because he threatened to take the kingdom away from Solomon.

"The Lord has confirmed me and placed me on the throne of my father, David; he has established my dynasty as he promised. So as surely as the Lord lives, Adonijah will die this very day!" So King Solomon ordered Benaiah son of Jehoiada

> to execute him, and Adonijah was put to
> death. (1 Kings 2:24–25 NLT)

Second, there would be sexual calamity through David's
household:

> Thus says the Lord, "Behold, I will raise
> up evil against you out of your own house;
> and I will take your wives before your
> eyes, and give them to your neighbor, and
> he shall lie with your wives in the sight of
> this sun. For you did it secretly; but I will
> do this thing before all Israel, and before
> the sun." (2 Samuel 12:11–12 RSV)

David's son Amnon raped his stepsister in 2 Samuel 13:14.
A few verses later, Absalom murdered Amnon because his
dad did nothing to avenge his sister. Later still, Absalom
slept with his father's concubines in public to insult him
and show himself better than his father to the whole
kingdom and the world:

> So they pitched a tent for Absalom upon
> the roof; and Absalom went in to his
> father's concubines in the sight of all
> Israel. (2 Samuel 16:22 RSV)

David repents, and God makes a promise to David—
through the prophet—of forgiveness and future hope.

> David said to Nathan, "I have sinned
> against the Lord." And Nathan said to
> David, "The Lord also has put away
> your sin; you shall not die." (2 Samuel
> 12:13 RSV)

Even though David repents, God gives David a third consequence. The child born to David and Bathsheba from their adultery would die:

> Nevertheless, because by this deed you
> have utterly scorned the Lord, the child
> that is born to you shall die. (2 Samuel
> 12:14 RSV)

The baby dies, which gives David and Bathsheba great grief and sadness. Interestingly, it is from God's amazing grace that their union later brings forth another son. From the lineage of Solomon, the wisest king ever, would come Jesus Christ.

God sometimes uses suffering and pain—just as a good parent would—to get our attention and leave a strong reminder not to commit that sin again. We may not like it, but it is from His loving hand. He is especially hard on Christian leaders.

CHAPTER 7

Something More

It is interesting that people first see suffering as punishment. In the Bible, Job suffered even though he was a righteous man who made God proud. Satan, of course, said Job was only a good boy because God provided him with everything. Take it away from him, God, and you will see he'll be different. When Job got hit with the loss of everything, his friends came to console him. They all seemed to think—and even taunted Job with the idea—that he must have done something wrong. "God is punishing you for something so quit being a pompous jerk and clean up your act!" they said. However, that was not true. Job was righteous! God said it!

> The Lord said to Satan, "Have you considered My servant Job? For there is no one like him on the earth, a blameless and upright man, fearing God and turning away from evil." (Job 1:8 RSV)

There is, however, another reason suffering comes. This reason takes deep spiritual understanding of God's eternal character to appreciate. It is seen in the healing of a man born blind:

> As He passed by, He saw a man blind from birth. And His disciples asked Him, "Rabbi, who sinned, this man or his parents, that he would be born blind?" (John 9:1–2 RSV)

Can you imagine the scorn, ostracism, and sadness this boy and his family experienced as he was growing up blind? The community assumed his blindness was a punishment for sin of his own doing or—more than likely—his parents' sin.

> Jesus answered, "It was neither that this man sinned, nor his parents; but it was so that the works of God might be displayed in him." (John 9:3 NASV)

The blind man had experienced a life full of suffering, ostracism, and stigma to give glory to the Lord.

Jesus was right because this incident exposed him as the Messiah sent from God and not a charlatan like the itinerant healers who used trickery to gain money and followers. No, Jesus's healing was the real deal. The man had been born blind and had remained so for years. He was no prop or con artist. He was a real, authentic blind person who everyone knew.

The healing even forced the religious establishment to look at Jesus in a different light. After the man was healed, he was called in and questioned about it. Throughout his testimony, he glorified the Lord to the religious leaders.

> The man answered and said to them, "Well, here is an amazing thing, that you do not know where He is from, and yet He opened my eyes. We know that God does not hear sinners; but if anyone is God-fearing and does His will, He hears him. Since the beginning of time it has never been heard that anyone opened the eyes of a person born blind. If this man were not from God, He could do nothing." (John 9:30–33 NASV)

They go back to the old paradigm to hide from dealing with the truth in front of their eyes about Jesus:

> They answered him, "You were born entirely in sins, and are you teaching us?" So they put him out. (John 9:34 NASV)

They couldn't handle the truth about what Jesus did, and they threw the healed man out of their chambers.

Can you imagine what special joy today—after two thousand years—this man who suffered all his childhood and a portion of his adulthood blind is experiencing along with all the other great saints who have suffered for the Lord and now enjoy Him forever?

Paul was brutally beaten within the last breath of his life. He was shipwrecked and imprisoned near the end of his life. In all of this, though, he did not complain. Paul sees the bigger purpose that is more important than his happiness or comfort in this life.

> Now I want you to know, brethren, that my circumstances have turned out for the greater progress of the gospel, so that my imprisonment in *the cause of* Christ has become well known throughout the whole praetorian guard and to everyone else, and that most of the brethren, trusting in the Lord because of my imprisonment, have far more courage to speak the word of God without fear. (Philippians 1:12–14 NASV)

Joseph was also a prime example of someone in the Bible who had a series of hurtful, bad, and evil things thrown his way. However, by faith, he recognized that they weren't just happenstances, bad luck, or karma. He saw it in a different perspective. His brothers hated and despised him because they thought he was a cocky, spoiled little brother because of his dad's favoritism. However, that was all a part of God's plan for him. Their feelings of hatred and jealousy festered, and they hatched an evil plan.

We meet Joseph at seventeen years of age, tattling on his brothers. Scripture tells us his dad favored him and even made him a special coat. Because of this, his brothers treated Joseph with contempt. However, Joseph starts to receive dreams:

> And when he told it to his brothers, they hated him even more. He said to them, "Please listen to this dream which I have had; for behold, we were binding sheaves in the field, and lo, my sheaf rose up and also stood erect; and behold, your sheaves gathered around and bowed down to my sheaf." Then his brothers said to him, "Are you actually going to reign over us? Or are you really going to rule over us?" So they hated him even more for his dreams and for his words. (Genesis 37:6–8 NASV)

He shared a similar dream with his dad and his brothers that didn't go over well. It even shocked his dad. However, God was revealing to all of them what was going to happen in God's grand plan to save Israel.

The plot thickens when Joseph is sent by his dad to check on the welfare of his brothers as they were tending the family sheep. It was their opportunity to get rid of Joseph for good. First, they plot to kill him and tell their dad a wild animal killed him.

Ruben speaks up for Joseph and spares him from murder. His idea was to leave him in the pit to die of natural causes. Secretly, Ruben was planning to come back and rescue Joseph later. They acted on their plan, but while they were eating, Judah proposed making a profit on him and selling him as a slave to the Ishmaelites:

> Then some Midianite traders passed by, so
> they pulled *him* up and lifted Joseph out of
> the pit, and sold him to the Ishmaelites for
> twenty *shekels* of silver. Thus they brought
> Joseph into Egypt. (Genesis 37:28 NASV)

The brothers go back and tell their father that Joseph was eaten by the wild animals, and they give him Joseph's bloody coat as evidence.

The Midianites sold Joseph "in Egypt to Potiphar, Pharaoh's officer, the captain of the bodyguard" (Genesis 37:36 NASV).

Joseph was very good at what he did and took a lot off the plate of his master. Joseph was so successful that he was put in charge of pretty much everything:

> So he left everything he owned in Joseph's
> charge; and with him *there* he did not
> concern himself with anything except the
> food which he ate. (Genesis 37:39:6a)

But Joseph was also "handsome in form and appearance" (Genesis 39:6b NASV), which was a problem:

> It came about after these events that his
> master's wife looked with desire at Joseph,
> and she said, "Lie with me." (Genesis 39:7
> NASV)

He did what was right in the eyes of his master and God. He refused her "day after day" (Genesis 39:10 NASV).

She was not going to take his refusals as an answer. She even grabbed him and tried to pull him into bed, but he pulled away from her, leaving his cloak behind (Genesis 39:12). He left his garment in her hand and fled outside, and she falsely accused him. When his boss came home, Joseph was sent to jail (Genesis 39:16–18 NASV).

Joseph went to jail, but he continued to walk with the Lord. God was with him even though he was jailed unjustly:

> But the Lord was with Joseph and extended kindness to him, and gave him favor in the sight of the chief jailer. (Genesis 39:21 NASV)

He practically ran the jail and met a baker and cupbearer. His interpretations of their dreams were spot-on. Even though the cupbearer promised to remind the king about Joseph, he remained in prison for several more years. The cupbearer forgot him:

> For I was in fact kidnapped from the land of the Hebrews, and even here I have done nothing that they should have put me into the dungeon. (Genesis 40:15 NASV)

Two years later, Pharaoh had a dream that no one could interpret. The cupbearer remembered Joseph's interpretation:

Now a Hebrew youth was with us there,
a servant of the captain of the bodyguard,
and we related them to him, and he
interpreted our dreams for us. To each
one he interpreted according to his own
dream. (Genesis 41:12 NASV)

Joseph is cleaned up and brought in to meet with the Pharaoh. He explains the meaning of the dream. A great famine is to come on Egypt. Joseph suggests how to prepare for the famine. Joseph's plan is so good that Pharaoh recognizes Joseph and makes him second-in-command to him (Genesis 41:38–41). It was a long road for Joseph, from seventeen to thirty years of age, to be before Pharaoh. He was to fulfill the fourteen-year plan God supplied in the dream. He first built up stores of grain for seven years to supply Egypt and the surrounding nations with food during the seven-year famine that came.

He executed the plan, and it worked well. One group that needed food was his family. His brothers came to him and bowed before him, fulfilling his prophecy (Genesis 37:5–8). His brothers didn't recognize him, but through their two visits, Joseph saw a difference in his brothers. When Joseph finally revealed himself to them, it was emotionally overwhelming for him, and his brothers were filled with fear and guilt:

Joseph hurried *out* for he was deeply
stirred over his brother, and he sought *a
place* to weep; and he entered his chamber
and wept there. (Genesis 43:30 NASV)

He wept so loudly that the Egyptians heard *it*, and the household of Pharaoh heard *of it*. Then Joseph said to his brothers, "I am Joseph! Is my father still alive?" But his brothers could not answer him, for they were dismayed at his presence. Then Joseph said to his brothers, "Please come closer to me." And they came closer. And he said, "I am your brother Joseph, whom you sold into Egypt. Now do not be grieved or angry with yourselves, because you sold me here, for God sent me before you to preserve life. For the famine *has been* in the land these two years, and there are still five years in which there will be neither plowing nor harvesting. God sent me before you to preserve for you a remnant in the earth, and to keep you alive by a great deliverance." (Genesis 45:2–7 NASV)

Here is a golden nugget. Look at Joseph's perspective on all those bad experiences. The long and enduring spree of bad and good events, as Joseph saw it, were all purposely ordained. God sent and directed them for the deliverance of His people.

Chapter 8

Where Do We Go from Here?

We have been through a good cross section of the scriptures concerning suffering, but we have left out a critical factor: the character of God. That is where the real challenge comes to our thinking and faith. We reason that if God is love (1 John 4:8; Romans 5:8; John 3:16), then why would He allow or even cause these things to happen? He is sovereign (Psalm 115:3; Psalm 135:6; Isaiah 46:11) and in control of everything. Nothing catches Him by surprise! Even Satan cannot do things without His say so (Luke 22:31; Job 1:12; Revelation 20:7). Therefore, we ask, "Why?" or "How could He?"

Here is where our faith in God is really stretched. There are several characteristics or attributes of God that put Him in a league of His own (Isaiah 44:6). God is omniscient or all-knowing. His knowledge has no limits (Psalm 147:4–5). He knows the events of our lives (Genesis 45:5) and the finite parts of our bodies

(Matthew 10:30). He knew us "before the foundation of the world" (Ephesians 1:4 NASV) and "in our mother's womb" (Psalm 139:1–11 NIV). From the beginning to the end, scripture is replete with His knowledge of all things (Isaiah 46:9; Isaiah 57:15; Revelation 1:8). God is also infinitely wise (Job 12:13; Romans 16:27) in knowing and understanding far beyond our wisdom (Isaiah 46:10).

During his suffering and dealing with friends who tried to comfort him, Job states what he knows intellectually about God (Job 28:12–28). In the end of the chapter, his creedal statement is correct:

> And this is what he says to all humanity:
> "The fear of the Lord is true wisdom; to
> forsake evil is real understanding." (Job
> 28:28 NLT)

In the next three chapters, Job goes over the events in his life and recites his belief. However, his friends are still convinced something is wrong with Job for God to let this happen. It seems, by God's response to Job, that maybe Job's heart and emotions are catching up to what he knows by faith to be true. Job wants either judgment or vindication from God.

God questions Job on how much he knows about what God has done and does (Job 38–41 NLT). Job responds briefly—in total humbleness—to the wisdom and work of God (Job 40:3–5 NLT). God continues to show Job more of His work and wisdom, and Job responds that God is God and he is not (Job 42:3–4 NLT).

In this life, we don't have all the answers. At times, we may think we know, but that is not the case:

> We see things imperfectly as in a cloudy mirror, but then we will see everything with perfect clarity. All that I know now is partial and incomplete, but then I will know everything completely, just as God now knows me completely. (1 Corinthians 13:12 NLT)

As we see with Job, this is not a fairy tale in which we go off and live happily ever after. Life is not like that. God doubly restores the things of this life to Job, but He never fully answers the question of why. The loss is still there. It's not the same, but as we learn from the experiences of Job and others in the scriptures, it is not necessary for us to know why.

God's ways are different from our ways (Isaiah 55:8–11). Things come about under His oversight for many reasons and purposes that we don't understand on this side of eternity. What we do know is that He does everything from His perfect and pure wisdom. Like Job, the only thing necessary is our relationship with Him by faith. We can live without the why, but we can't live without Him. The journey of faith is knowing that we have a God we trust—and He is bigger and wiser than we are. He knows our circumstances and exactly what we need now and in eternity. He is the only thing necessary for this life and eternity.

A colleague of mine experienced a tragic event that evidenced this kind of faith in God. He was driving down a two-lane highway where a small motel stood just over a hill. As he came over the ridge where the motel driveway intersected the road, the owner's little son pedaled his bike into the middle of the highway—in a direct line with my friend's car. He hit the child head-on, killing him. The trauma to all was overwhelming.

That night, as he sat overcome in his home, he received a call from the boy's mother. He expressed his sorrow, but she comforted him with her own faith. She explained that this event was ordained by God and, for some reason unknown to her or anyone on this earth, the Lord had called her son to heaven. She knew God had a plan, and she didn't blame my friend for what had happened. She said that someday they would all know why it had been God's plan to call her son home that day. This woman's tremendous faith in God allowed her to trust in the Lord's "big picture" beyond her own deep personal pain. That faith gives Him glory. On this side of eternity, she will never know the answer to why, but she willingly trusts in Him, the one who does!

> Oh, how great are God's riches and wisdom and knowledge! How impossible it is for us to understand his decisions and his ways! For who can know the Lord's thoughts? Who knows enough to give him advice? And who has given him so much that he needs to pay it back? For

everything comes from him and exists by his power and is intended for his glory. All glory to him forever! Amen. (Romans 11:33–36 NLT)

BIBLIOGRAPHY

Barclay, William. *The Master's Men: Character Sketches of the Disciples.* Nashville, TN: Abingdon Press, 1993.

Kushner, Harold S. *Why Bad Things Happen to Good People.* New York: Schocken Books, 1981.

The Bible, The New American Standard Version (NASV).

The Bible, The New International Version (NIV).

The Bible, The New Living Translation (NLT).

The Bible, The Revised Standard Bible (RSV).

Printed in the United States
By Bookmasters